G O O

Tee Jay Woods
Foreward By Pastor Canton Jones

Copyright © 2024 by Tee Jay Woods Ministries

All rights reserved. No part of this book may be reproduced in any form without permission from the author, except as permitted by U.S. copyright law.

To request permission, contact:

Travis L. Woods, Jr.
10221 Krause Road
Suite 81
Chesterfield, VA 23832
www.teejaywoods.com

Back cover design by
Salt And Light Media Production Company
Editing by Chaya Braxton
Formatting by Mechelle Luster

DEDICATION

First, I would like to thank my Lord and Savior, Jesus Christ! God.

Thank you for sending Jesus to the cross and resurrecting Him so I could be redeemed.

I am profoundly grateful to my loving wife, Latarsha Woods, and our three beautiful daughters, Destiny, Trinity, and Serenity Woods. Their unwavering love and support have been my guiding light throughout this writing journey. Their presence in my life has not only inspired my writing but has also shaped me into the man, husband, and father I am today.

I would also like to thank my father, the late Elder Travis L. Woods, Sr., for showing me unconditional love as a father, leading me to Jesus, and continuing to show me Jesus until his transition.

I want to express my heartfelt gratitude to my stepmother, Pastor Janet Woods, aka Ma Janet, who played multiple roles and cared for my dad for many years. I am also thankful to my stepfather, Gary, and my mother, Sylvia Carter, for their contributions in shaping who I am. You two have been there when others weren't, and I am grateful for you!

I would like to thank my first pastor, Phillip E. Knight, Sr. from Rockhill Baptist Church, who preached and sang the Gospel of Jesus Christ every week during service. I am also grateful for my first spiritual father, Apostle Steve I. Foreman, and his wife, Lady Olivia Foreman, from Abundant Life Church of Christ, who groomed me in ministry. They taught me how to dig into the Word of God and how to live by what I read.

Lastly, I want to acknowledge the profound influence of my spiritual father and pastor, Bishop Daniel Robertson, Jr., and his lovely wife, Co-Pastor Elena Robertson. Your teachings ignited a fire in me to spread the message of hope in Jesus Christ to the world.

The oil that is on your life, I was able to flow under the self-same anointing to write this book!

FOREWARD

BY PASTOR CANTON JONES

I met Tee Jay seventeen years ago at a youth conference hosted by his church. That was right around when my first daughter, Love, was born—she is nineteen now, and I'm the proud parent of four, while Tee Jay's got three of his own. That should tell you how long we have been connected. From the jump, Tee Jay and I clicked. His down-to-earth vibe and realness drew me in. Tee Jay was genuine and truly cared about the kids in his community. It was clear that he was a father to many. Given all of that, it's no shock Tee Jay's first book is called "The Good Father."

Over the years, I have seen firsthand how Tee Jay's commitment to his community and his role as a father left a lasting impression. In our ministry circles, folks often talk about money, prosperity, and making it big. But Tee Jay? He chose a different lane; Tee Jay kept it real, sharing his story from a place of vulnerability and touching on topics most men keep locked up inside. In our friendship and brotherhood, his advice was a breath of fresh air because it wasn't about flashy success but about being a kingdom servant.

Through his storytelling, Tee Jay is honest about his own life experiences and struggles, offering strength, encouragement, and hope to other men facing similar battles. From the very beginning of "The Good Father," we see him go through unemployment, bouts of humiliation, moments of triumph, and his many encounters with Jesus. Tee Jay's book guides others, showing that real success is rooted in the love and care we give to our kids and communities. Dedication to family and devotion to faith are at the core of his message. In his work, Tee Jay teaches us that being a "Good Father" and a good man is about more than bouncing back; it is about transforming into a strong, loving father—against all odds. Being a "Good Father" also isn't about perfection or chasing material things; it's about having integrity, and willingness to grow and learn from our experiences.

In this digital age, where so many people are trapped in their social media accounts, constantly scrolling and searching for validation, Tee Jay remains a disruptor. He is the reachable, touchable parent who nurtures everyone with his warm, comforting presence. Tee Jay is not concerned about the "likes or followers"; he's about authentic, meaningful connections and making a difference in the lives of others.

In "The Good Father," I encourage you to journey with Tee Jay and use it as a roadmap. His insights and experiences provide valuable lessons on the importance of fatherhood, the power of vulnerability, and the strength that comes from faith and perseverance. This book is truly for anyone striving to be a better father, husband, or man.

PREFACE

In January 2024, during a Daniel fast, I felt a prompting from God to write this book. My initial reaction was disbelief—me, write a book? But God's guidance was clear: name it "The Good Father," drawing from the lessons I had shared with incarcerated men during my jail ministry. A week later, while brushing my teeth on a Sunday morning, the Lord spoke again: "Release it on Father's Day." Despite my skepticism, I obeyed, marking the start of this journey.

I've been blessed with several father figures, most notably my late father, Elder Travis Woods, Sr. Though he was not a perfect man, he was perfect for me. His transformation from a man of the streets to a man of faith shaped me profoundly. My dad's discipline and wisdom left an unforgettable mark on me. We lived three hours away from one another, but he could send correction in a way that would instantly cause me to straighten up. His words of wisdom captivated my heart every time he spoke. That is why losing him a couple years ago was difficult and bittersweet. I am very clear that my father passed his mantle to me to finish the work he started for the next generation of fathers. While I am grateful for how he taught me to pray with expectation, worship without restriction, and humble myself before God, I have to be honest: I miss him.

In 2011, I met my other father—my spiritual father—when my family and I joined Mt. Gilead Full Gospel International Ministries in Chesterfield, Virginia—one of the most wonderful churches on this side of heaven! Our fierce leader and pastor, Bishop Daniel Robertson, Jr., truly taught us how to be disciples of Christ. From Bishop, I have learned how to balance ministry and family. His children even witness this when they talk about him; all his children serve in ministry and have amazing families. Like my own father, Bishop is a real-life inspiration who provided me with spiritual guidance.

"The Good Father" is a call to the fatherly role models out there whose love is needed and whose wisdom is valued; your presence is irreplaceable. "The Good Father" is an appeal for you to step out of hiding and embrace the profound impact you can have on families around you. For those who may have forgotten or doubt they know how to be a parent to their children, remember that God is the ultimate "Good Father," His love knows no bounds, and His gifts are endless. So, to every father out there, know that your role is significant, you are cherished, and your influence is immeasurable. Shine your light, for many children eagerly await your guidance and love.

Even when
the unexpected
happens,
a "Good Father"
keeps his trust
in God.

CHAPTER 1

THE UNEXPECTED

I remember it just like it was yesterday. It was January 2014, a cold winter day, and the first time I felt relief from overcoming the challenges I had experienced the year before. My heart was set on having a great year, but I was unprepared for what would happen next. I received a call from my supervisor, who asked me to come into the office for an impromptu meeting—in the dead winter—during what was supposed to be family time. It was around Christmas time, and the office was closed, so being called for a meeting was not a good sign.

My wife and I put on our clothes to take the trip to the office. She was seven months pregnant with our daughter, Trinity Faith, so during this season, it took her a little longer to get dressed than usual. My wife and I were at peace as we traveled in the car. Honestly, we weren't thinking about the upcoming meeting. We discussed different things without the thought that this meeting would change our lives.

As we arrived at the facility, my wife said she would stay in the car. I did not feel anxious or afraid as I walked across the parking lot. Although I wondered why they wanted to meet with me, that thought lasted a few seconds. I walked into the empty building and greeted my supervisor and the clinical supervisor on staff. We sat down and they began to discuss my performance on the job. They told me I did not handle a few incidents particularly well. As they talked, I just listened; it felt like their words were echoing off the wall.

After the end of our discussion, they fired me. Right on the spot! Meanwhile, my seven-month pregnant wife was in the car waiting for me to finish the meeting. As I left the meeting to return to my car, I thought, "I just got fired, and my wife is gonna be so upset."

All I could do at that point was pray. As we were preparing to leave the parking lot, my wife asked, "How did the meeting go?" I took a deep breath, looked at her, and replied with those awful words, "They fired me."

"I know," my wife said very calmly. Her faith was unshakeable.

"You know?" I responded, mimicking her.

"Yes, I know," she said. "I was praying for you during the meeting, and God showed me they were going to fire you," said my wife.

I was so shocked by how much peace she had. I knew God had things under control at that point, but my thoughts and feelings were everywhere. My mind was racing; all I could think about was how the company didn't fire just ME alone; they fired my entire family, including our baby.

Thoughts began to race through my mind, "How in the world will I be able to afford what is about to happen?" As I talked to God in my mind, I asked God what was going on. I told Him everything I did for the company as if He didn't already know.

I bet God was laughing at me, saying, "Boy, do you know who I am? I am the God of the universe!"

Amidst this new turmoil, one thing became abundantly clear to me—God's plan, though mysterious, was unfolding before us. And so, with faith as our compass, we ventured into the unknown, ready to weather whatever storms may come. That was my first experience of having to put TOTAL trust in God.

The bottom line is that,
as a father,
you naturally desire
to provide
for your family.

This is a natural instinct
that all men have
inside of them.

Yes, all men have
this in their DNA,
but not every man
demonstrates it.

CHAPTER 2

THE PRESSURES OF BEING A FATHER

The next morning, sunlight filtered through my bedroom curtains. I woke up, but I wasn't leaving for work or saying goodbye to my family. Instead, a sea of worries engulfed me. All I could think about was the fact that I was a husband and father—the breadwinner of our household. My five-year-old daughter, Destiny Grace Woods, attended an expensive private Christian school, and I had another daughter on the way! The reality of losing my job began to set in.

You see, from the very beginning, God gave man a huge responsibility. It's written in

Genesis 2:15 (KJV), "And the Lord God took the man, and put him into the garden of Eden to dress it and to keep it." So, when God created Adam, He gave him the task of tending to the garden, which became a part of Adam's identity.

Working is a natural part of who we are as men—it is woven into our very being. Consequently, there's immense pressure placed on a man when he can't provide for his family. I've felt this pressure, and it's hard to put into words just how intense it can be.

A sense of pride and fulfillment comes from a man's ability to provide for his family. As 2 Thessalonians 3:10 (KJV) states, "For even when we were with you, this we commanded you, that if any would not work, neither should he eat." If the act of working determines whether one should eat, it's like choosing between life and death. So, work then, becomes extremely important. This conviction is something every man, whether they're a believer or not, should have. I believe God, in His infinite wisdom, has placed this conviction in every man's heart as a natural law, inspiring them to work diligently.

As I sat there, the devil toyed with my emotions, stirring up feelings of anger, sadness, frustration, and bitterness toward my supervisor and the company leaders. They knew my wife was seven months pregnant! How could they fire me after everything I'd done for the company for the past eight years? To make matters worse, this happened right after Christmas. I couldn't believe it. The pressure mounted as I replayed the situation over and over in my mind.

Thoughts of inadequacy flooded my mind, telling me I was worthless, that I would never find another job, and that my career was ruined because everyone would find out I'd been fired. I felt certain that nobody would ever trust me again, and I was on the brink of giving up. I felt like going into hiding. As I sat on the loveseat in my beautiful home, I wrestled with inner turmoil.

The bottom line is that as a father, your natural instinct is to provide for your family. This is a drive all men should have, even if it's not always obvious. When under pressure, this drive can be conflicted by men who might revert to their primal instincts, following their fleshy desires or returning to familiar patterns. This is one reason why so many men, especially Black men, end up in jail—for selling drugs, stealing, committing violent crimes, and more.

The pressure of losing a job can undermine everything you've built if you let it. How you perceive the situation makes a big difference. You can see it as a devastating setback or as an opportunity to learn, mature, and grow.

Your wife might wonder, "Why doesn't my husband like to work?" Your partner or the mother of your child might wonder, "Why doesn't my child's father like to work?" You might even wonder, "Why don't I, as a man, like to work? Why doesn't my son, nephew, father, or brother like to work?" My answer is that God instilled a work ethic in them, but sometimes the challenges of the world can lead to feelings of discouragement. Society often promotes an "I don't care" attitude, but we need God Almighty to help us see things through a spiritual lens. Remember, our struggle isn't against flesh and blood. Focus on how God wants you to overcome this seemingly "impossible" situation.

A "Good Father" focuses on possibilities rather than defeat.

CHAPTER 3

THE TURN AROUND

After a week, something shifted! I said to myself, I have to do something about this. I thought, enough is enough! I spent so much time agonizing over my past mistakes, I realized I couldn't keep punishing myself for what I'd done wrong. I decided to open my heart to the possibility of redemption. As I did, God began speaking to me about my true identity in Him. He reminded me of all the good things I'd done for His kingdom.

God reminded me of who He created me to be versus what man thought of me or even what I thought of myself. He had to remind me that I was not perfect and that I would make mistakes. As I meditated on the new understanding of my identity and the positive impact I'd made on various programs and people, I realized God was healing me. This healing had to take place to prepare me for what God would instruct me to do next. He began to speak to me prophetically. He told me that He wanted me to take the Youth Impact Conference, our yearly event for all the youth in the city, to the next level!

God revealed to me that He was transforming Youth Impact into a business, and I was to use all the experience and connections I had gained over the years. When something in our lives unexpectedly ends (even though God knows beforehand), it's often because He is about to birth something new within us. As I sat on the couch, the enemy tried to attack me, but it was also the place where God began to reveal my destiny. My old church used to sing, "Hold to God's Unchanging Hand," but it wasn't until that moment that I truly understood what those words meant.

My confidence in God began to soar to new heights. It was as if God turned my head and said, "Do you know who you are?" Often, we forget our true identity when faced with significant trials. We can get caught up in our natural selves, which can lead to destructive outcomes. Our natural tendencies can compromise who God created us to be. The flesh tries to suffocate our spirit, pushing us to abandon the process God is using to shape us. This is why David says in Psalm 51:10, "Create in me a clean heart, O God; and renew a right spirit within me." We must rebuke the spirits of depression, self-doubt, and low self-esteem. We need to embrace the right spirit that God is trying to release to us, which will take authority over every other spirit that tries to occupy us without permission.

When I recognized what was happening I realized that God was turning everything around (watch this) WITHIN ME FIRST! The transformation had to begin internally before it manifested in the physical world. God's voice changed the trajectory of my situation. When He spoke to me, it erased all my faults and renewed my faith in His Word. While reflecting on my circumstances, I asked God to forgive any wrongs I had done, and I forgave anyone who had hurt me during the process. I had to release them and move on. We must understand that God can turn everything around, but we need to follow certain principles to experience this change. Forgiveness is a key principle required to receive redemption and transformation. Where bitterness can block what God wants to do in your life, forgiveness will open many doors.

A "Good Father" seeks mentorship and counsel, because in the multitude of counselors, there is safety.

CHAPTER 4

MISCONCEPTIONS OF FATHERHOOD

There are many stigmas and misconceptions about fathers that have persisted over the years, especially in the Black community. While some of these stigmas are based on the behaviors of certain fathers who haven't matured, it's important to recognize that men are not inherently terrible fathers. A man can choose to be free from guilt and shame, allowing him to move forward from past mistakes. By seeking forgiveness from others, forgiving themselves, and forgiving those who have wronged them, they can strive to be good fathers today and in the future. We can either support those fathers who genuinely want to improve or let them struggle alone. Ultimately, it is the children who suffer the most when fathers are left to drown.

I am positive that you won't hear a father confessing, "Yeah, I want to be a terrible dad." It is highly unlikely. You won't find it! Most men aspire to be good fathers but struggle to model "Good Father" behavior, which indicates underlying mental, emotional, physical, and spiritual challenges. It may be because that father's role model is nowhere to be found. I'm not excusing negative behavior patterns, which is exactly why the current state of fatherhood is lacking. These fathers never underwent personal development, yet they find themselves with paternal responsibilities. This devastating cycle will persist unless we intervene decisively, starting now!

The misconception is that fathers want to be good dads, but many don't know how. Often, pride gets in the way, which leads them to avoid seeking guidance or advice. Proverbs 11:14 (KJV) wisely says, "Where there is no counsel, the people fall; but in the multitude of counselors there is safety." We all benefit from mentorship and guidance, which provide crucial accountability. I always emphasize that with accountability, behavior can improve! It's very likely that those who struggle with negative fatherhood behavior lack high accountability.

Fathers must understand that they play a crucial role in protecting the next generation. The devil seeks to destroy, and he may even use parents to do his bidding. As Jesus said in John 10:10 (KJV), "The thief cometh not, but for to steal, and to kill, and to destroy: I am come that they might have life, and that they might have it more abundantly." As fathers, we must be vigilant and shield our children from anything that could harm them.

The best way I can protect my children is through knowledge, wisdom, and spiritual principles. As my children hearken (listening with the intent to obey) to the spiritual wisdom and revelation God shares with me, this instantly transforms their lives. Then I get a front-row seat to see how the impartation I gave them plays out in their lives. See, the thief (satan) has a goal to separate fathers from their Heavenly Father so they cannot get downloads from the throne room of Heaven, which will ultimately transform generations to come. We must get into our rightful positions to hear from our Heavenly Father so that we can, in turn, share these downloads with our children.

Of all the men
in the world,
God picked <u>you</u> to be
the father of your children.

What an honor.

What a responsibility!

CHAPTER 5

RESPONSIBILITY

When I was let go from my job, I sought guidance from one of my financial mentors. He reminded me that my children did not ask to come into this world, and no matter what I was going through, I was responsible for their care. This profound statement resonated with me deeply. The responsibility of raising children belongs to parents; it belongs to fathers.

As fathers, we must acknowledge the divine privilege bestowed upon us. Out of all the men in this vast world, the Divine chose us to be the fathers of our children. This is not a responsibility to be taken lightly. The Creator of the universe has entrusted us with this sacred assignment. When we allow our personal issues to overshadow our role as fathers, we betray this privilege, displaying a selfish and immature mindset.

The foundation of being a "Good Father" is understanding that your life is not yours! The goal of this book is that the "Good Father" who is rooted in you (that God instilled in you) will come forth and manifest! The father must be the most selfless person in the household. We must demonstrate the same characteristics as God, our Heavenly Father. God "gave" his only begotten son, Jesus, for everyone, including you. So, as a "Good Father," you must be a giver. You can't be selfish as a "Good Father" because selfishness means you're living in direct opposition to God's very nature!

Let's be honest: in many cases, it is OUR fault that we have gained a negative stigma around fatherhood. I say this because I'm in there with you as a father. I understand and support you. But today, it is time for all of us to make a shift. We all have made mistakes as a father, but today, we choose to be a "Good Father" and eventually a "Great Father!" We should never plan to stay on the same level. As a "Good Father," we must plan to make the necessary daily adjustments to go to the next level in fatherhood. We can't afford to make the same mistakes!

The first step to transformation is for "you" to take responsibility for your actions. Without taking responsibility, repairing broken relationships becomes impossible. Your actions may have damaged your relationships with others. It's time to mature and accept responsibility. That means forgiving others, asking for forgiveness, and forgiving yourself. Even if your apology isn't accepted, make the effort to seek forgiveness. Then, let go and move forward. Forgiving yourself is essential to breaking free from guilt and shame.

A "Good Father" understands that without accountability, behavior won't change.

CHAPTER 6

ACCOUNTABILITY

I often say, "Without accountability, behavior won't change." Intentionally placing myself in accountable situations enables me to pursue success deliberately. Have you ever heard the world-renowned author and entrepreneur Jim Rohn say, "Whoever you hang around with is who you become?" I surround myself with strong, credible, and mature fathers to deepen my understanding of fatherhood. I strongly desire accountability, which marks the initial steps toward becoming a "Good Father."

When you desire accountability, it compels you to change any behaviors that are contrary to being a "Good Father." That is why I recommend that every father have a mentor or someone they can glean from with a credible history of fatherhood. The goal of this relationship is for you to learn and be empowered as a father. The accountability aspect ensures you stay on course toward the goal of being the "Good Father" God desires you to be.

We should desire what God desires. We need accountability to become who He wants us to be as fathers. We all need a role model to teach us how to navigate fatherhood. That underscores the importance of being accountable to someone for success. My cousin, Pastor Trev Evans, often says, "We were not made to do life alone." This truth resonates with me deeply. As fathers, we need accountability to thrive.

I define accountability as the obligation or willingness to accept responsibility for one's actions, decisions, and behaviors. It involves being accountable to oneself and others for the outcomes of those actions and decisions.

American radio personality, comedian, producer, and motivational speaker, Willie Moore, Jr. uses the acronym H.O.T. (Honest, Open, and Transparent) to describe a system of accountability. Being H.O.T. with a mentor or friend changes relationship dynamics, which fosters vulnerability and receptiveness. Your accountability partners should fearlessly remind you of your commitments, speak the truth, and help you align your actions with words. My children, along with my spiritual parents, keep me grounded through their accountability. Spiritual parents like Bishop Daniel Robertson, Jr. and Co-Pastor Elena Robertson are invaluable. They speak to my spirit, guiding me to align my flesh with God's Word.

Spiritual growth requires accountability, and I desire it earnestly. Accountability has saved my life! Matthew 7:13-14 warns against the broad path of destruction and encourages the narrow path of life. Embracing accountability helps us stay focused and discerning, seeking guidance only from those appointed by God. Let's embrace accountability to fulfill our calling as good fathers.

Being a "Good Father" is not an anthem, but it is a lifestyle.

CHAPTER 7

GOOD FATHER CHARACTERISTIC: PROTECTOR

There are essential characteristics of goodness that you ought to embody as a father.

Just saying you are a "Good Father" is not what I am encouraging. Instead, I advocate for understanding the expectations, mentally adopting the characteristics, and then embodying what you have adopted. Just saying you are a "Good Father" can be empty words with no action, but being one without saying is what carries weight. Because of shame, intimidation, insecurity, guilt, and so many other challenges, men sometimes feel they have to prove themselves as a father. Remember that being a "Good Father" is not an anthem but a lifestyle.

Let's start with being a protector—you know, someone who looks out for others. According to Merriam-Webster Dictionary, a protector cares for its kingdom, but for us dads, it's about keeping our children safe. It's like an instinct. We want to shield our kids from harm. But here's the thing: being a protector isn't just about physical stuff like fighting off danger. It's about more than that. It's about giving our kids inner strength, like a spiritual backbone. Because in today's world, it's not just about what's outside that's scary; it's also about what's inside. If our kids don't have that inner strength, that resilience, they could easily get knocked around by all the craziness out there. So, let's focus on building them up from the inside out. That way, they'll have the tools to handle whatever life throws their way. The world is so wicked that without the necessary internal spiritual fortitude needed in this day and time, your children can easily fall victim.

Protect your children by building up their minds, souls, and spirits! The most important of these is their spirit. When you strengthen their spiritual side, it will guide everything else. Yes, your kids need a strong intellect and soul, but a strong spirit will bring them supernatural wisdom and a healthy soul. Their spirit will also encourage their body to follow the Word of God. As they desire to follow the Word, everything else will fall into place. So, focus on speaking the Word of God into their spirit and watch how God builds them from the inside out.

Teaching your children to navigate this challenging world by empowering them and modeling godly behavior is the best protection for your family. When kids develop a strong conviction about their daily behavior, it changes them from the inside out. As fathers, our role isn't to control our children but to equip them and let them make their own decisions as they grow in the Lord. Remember, the Bible says, "Train up a child in the way he should go: and when he is old, he will not depart from it" (Proverbs 22:6 KJV). So, focus on instilling these values early on and trust that they will stay rooted as they mature.

As I was writing this book, I witnessed firsthand what I'm describing in this chapter. One Saturday night, my wife, Latarsha, and I went out to a restaurant for a date. We ordered appetizers and, for some reason, we took longer than usual to decide on our main entrees. While we were enjoying our appetizers and having a great conversation, my wife received a call from our oldest daughter, Destiny, who was babysitting our two youngest daughters, Trinity and Serenity. Destiny told us that Serenity got hurt while playing with her older sister, Trinity. We had specifically instructed them to shower and lie down before watching a movie, but things didn't go as planned. All I could hear over the phone was my 6-year-old daughter screaming at the top of her lungs, "JESUS, JESUS, JESUS!"

We left the restaurant immediately and rushed home. As soon as we entered the house, we found our daughter crying and saying her lip was busted. It was swollen, and there was a cut on the inside of her top lip. We quickly decided to take her to the emergency room to check if she needed stitches. But before leaving, we wanted to have a quick talk with Trinity, our 9-year-old, to find out what happened. When we entered Trinity's room, we found her sitting on her bed, crying, praying, and reading her Bible. She was asking God for forgiveness because she knew she had disobeyed our instructions and felt responsible for what had happened.

This situation shows how God protects your children when they have their own personal relationship with Him. You might wonder how He protected them since Serenity got hurt. Yes, she was hurt, but she knew to call on "JESUS" for healing. Trinity knew to seek forgiveness from God. This moment was not just a lesson; it was a profound spiritual transformation for them.

Here are some tips of ways to empower your children spiritually:

1. Pray over your children and pray with them in the morning and at night. If you

can't pray with them during those times, teach them how to pray together so they can develop their relationships with God. Don't force them but model the behavior and encourage them to pray.
2. Throughout the day, play Christian worship music in your home, especially at night, while they are asleep in their rooms.
3. Discuss the meanings of scriptures with your children.
4. Attend weekly services at church.
5. Have fun and discuss their experience in children's church or the main sanctuary, if this applies.
6. Have open family discussions where your children can freely share their feelings about different situations. These discussions happen organically because of our bond, but sometimes, you must call a family meeting to discuss a specific topic.
7. Have your children repeat an affirmation before dropping them off at school and allow them to lead morning prayer.

8. Ultimately, keep things fun while learning about Jesus. The most important advice is to create an atmosphere that encourages your children to hunger for God.

A "Good Father" knows whatever you do for your family shouldn't take *away* from your family.

CHAPTER 8

GOOD FATHER CHARACTERISTIC: PROVIDER

One of God's names is Jehovah Jireh, meaning "God will provide" in Hebrew. I believe when God created man, He put this characteristic in him (man) because He (God) is a provider. I think providing for our family is a part of our nature. In Genesis 1:26 (KJV), the Word of God says: "And God said, Let us make man in our image, after our likeness: and let them have dominion over the fish of the sea, and over the fowl of the air, and the cattle, and all the earth, and over every creeping thing that creepeth upon the earth."

In other words, God has created us in His image and likeness. So, we should look and act like Him. That means we should display certain behaviors based on scripture. God is a good, "Good Father," and He provides for His children. Some fathers may desire to do the same thing but may not have the strength or know-how to do it as God would.

For example, I have talked to men who are incarcerated for selling drugs and stealing. Based on their confession, they did it to care for their children. Now, before you judge these men, I believe the desire was pure, but the action was contaminated. There are many reasons why these types of behavior are contaminated, but I genuinely believe the initial motive was pure. As a "Good Father," we cannot allow our motives to be contaminated with distractions; we must learn to do things God's way—with integrity. This is why I serve God and focus on honoring Him instead of doing my own thing.

One day, I was teaching a fatherhood class to a group of incarcerated men, and it finally hit them. Their eyes opened up. One of the gentlemen asked, "How in the world are we doing this *for* our family and children, yet it took us *away* from our children?" If you truly do something for your family, it shouldn't take you away from them! Instead, it should bring you closer together. We cannot allow the enemy to trick us with emotional bondage. The devil will try to attack you where you are most vulnerable, and he knows he can try to get you with your family, more specifically, your children. His ultimate goal is to kill, steal, and destroy you (John 10:10). Honestly, the devil doesn't just want you; he wants the next generation, which is your children. He wants to disrupt their destiny.

Previously, while working for the justice system, I encountered many individuals who became incarcerated due to trying to do something for their families. Still, the behavior and mindset took on a life of its own. Some men dig such a deep hole into a criminal lifestyle that started innocently. It becomes so bad; they don't know how to get out of it until something devastating happens. I am writing this book so men can get a hold of their lives right now or read it and say, "I am not going in that direction." That is my prayer!

If the truth be told, becoming a father is a blessing that can easily become a burden if you don't manage the weight of responsibility appropriately. Becoming a father is straight-up pressure because you feel the weight of your family on your shoulders. But God gives you grace as a father, making it much more manageable. I have seen men who don't embrace God's grace for fathers. Don't let that be you. Embrace it, receive it, and walk in it! If you have made mistakes, God has already forgiven you. Still, I encourage you to ask God to forgive you, according to 1 John 1:9, and ask the people affected by your bad decision to forgive you.

I have had many sessions with incarcerated men during fatherhood classes, and I saw firsthand how the pressures of life as a father overtook them. I want to encourage men to know that life as a father can and will be a blessing when you allow God to invade your life and mold you as a father. No one can show us how to be good fathers better than our God, Abba Father. I remember when my wife and I had our first baby girl, Destiny, and I was at church talking to one of the church leaders about how it felt to be a brand-new father. He already had three sons, and he told me something that I would never forget. He laughed and said, "You don't know how to be a father, but the Holy Ghost will help you. Just depend on the Holy Ghost, and He will lead and guide you." From that day until now, I have depended on the Holy Spirit to lead and guide me in raising my girls. That eases the pressure that comes along with being a "Good Father." The pressure may be there, but I declare it won't overtake me! When I pray in my heavenly language, I build up my faith, and God gives me instructions. I do all this because I truly desire to be a "Good Father."

I want to honor those men who are fabulous providers for their families! Those men work one, two, and sometimes three jobs to provide for their loved ones. I honor those dads who are present in their children's lives and understand they must make an impact in their homes before they can impact the world. Those fathers may have to overcome anxiety, depression, and demands from their wives, girlfriends, parents, church family, community members, baby mommas, etc. But I salute you, men, for holding down the fort day in and day out for your family—you ARE good fathers!

CHAPTER 9

GOOD FATHER CHARACTERISTIC: AFFIRMATIONS

An affirmation is a positive assertion or suggestion. To "affirm" someone also means to give them emotional support or encouragement. When I think about the word affirmation, I immediately think about my biological father, the late Elder Travis L. Woods, Sr. He was the epitome of giving affirmations! As I write this book, this chapter reminds me most of my father. He passed away in June 2022, and I get a little emotional because his affirmations shaped me as a man! I loved it when my father would affirm me; his affirmations gave me what felt like bursts of strength, energy, and hope to keep going. I felt like I could do anything—that anything was possible! His affirmations gave me breath, and I felt as if I was the only one who mattered at that moment. With his gold front tooth shining, my dad would grin at me and give me this look whenever he affirmed me.

Jesus said in John 6:63 (KJV), "It is the spirit that quickeneth; the flesh profiteth nothing: the words that I speak unto you, they are spirit, and they are life." Since we are joint heirs of Jesus Christ, our words should also be spirit and life. That is why it is so important to not just say whatever you want to your child. Your words are powerful! The Bible declares in Proverbs 18:21 (KJV), "Death and life are in the power of the tongue: and they that love it shall eat the fruit thereof." So, this means you can either speak life or death to your children. I encourage you to choose life!

It truly bothers me when I hear parents use curse words (profanity) towards their children. In my opinion, it is more standard now than ever before. That parent is either unaware of how deeply this affects their child, or they are ignorant and don't want to know. The old saying "sticks and stones may break my bones, but words will never hurt me" is a LIE! Some parents have cut off their children's destiny with their mouths. For instance, a child might see something that can change their entire life and start believing it will come true. When the parent says, "that would never happen for you," they may be speaking death to something that's alive in the child's life. As parents, we have to be slow to speak and quick to listen. The things we say can be detrimental to our children.

This type of behavior is a shame before God Almighty! As good fathers, we should always believe in our children as long as they're not believing for something that will harm them or someone else. Even if what they are believing is far-fetched and may not happen right away, don't knock down their vision or goal—instead, encourage it. Sometimes, as parents, we may not know if what our children are believing for is in God's will. When this happens, we can just pray about the situation. The Bible says in

Ephesians 6:4 (KJV), "And, ye fathers, provoke not your children to wrath: but bring them up in the nurture and admonition of the Lord." We shouldn't judge our children's situations based on our past mistakes or our current situation. I have seen God work miracles for my children just because they believe!

I will never forget as long as I live the way God moved on behalf of my oldest daughter, Destiny Grace Woods, in 2012. The year before, Destiny was walking around the house, playing with an imaginary dog named Fluffy. This was a daily routine for Destiny, and the more she played with Fluffy, the more she believed in having a dog of her own. In November, at a helps ministry meeting, my pastor, Bishop Daniel Robertson, Jr., declared that our church would pay off the remaining debt we owed on the church, which was 1.6 million dollars. He stated our first rally would be at the New Year's Eve Service, and he encouraged us to believe God for a financial seed to sow into the rally. So, my wife and I got a seed together and gave our seed. In the meantime, Destiny continued playing with her imaginary dog named Fluffy, but now she stated she desired a real dog. We encouraged her to pray for a dog, and she did that!

One day, I received a phone call from a friend who lived in New York City. He informed me that his mother-in-law had taken his dog—a shih tzu—and was on her way to North Carolina. The dog was in a bag on the bus, and it kept making noise. Suddenly, the bus made a stop in Richmond, VA. My friend's mother-in-law was told to take the dog off the bus and to the animal shelter. My friend asked if I could pick the dog up for him since I lived in Richmond. Then he said, "Honestly, man, my wife and I agreed that you can have the dog at no cost if you want. The dog is well-trained, and her name is Ari." I told him that my daughter had been believing God for a dog, and we praised God together! God supernaturally blessed us with a debt-free, well-trained dog that would normally have cost over $2,000—all because a three-year-old girl believed! And the church was paid off in 3 months and 1 week. Wow! Glory to God!

So, I encourage you to affirm your children every chance you get. Here are some examples of affirmations you can use:

- You are beautiful!
- You are handsome!
- You are smart!
- You have a beautiful smile.
- You can do anything you put your mind to.
- You are courageous.
- You are strong.
- You are loving.
- You are so helpful.
- You are so organized.
- You do an excellent job keeping your room clean.
- You will go a long way in life!
- You smell and look good!
- You have beautiful hair!
- You are so supportive.

I think you get the picture (lol)! The enemy wants us to speak down to our children, but it's so important for us to do the opposite. The last thing I will tell you in this chapter is to always use your manners toward your children—saying thank you, please, yes ma'am, and yes sir. When I respect my children in that manner, they automatically return the favor. It creates a culture of respect in our household when we use manners toward one another. I model this behavior for them to see, and it is immediately reciprocated. I also encourage you to speak what you want to see instead of what you currently see (if what you currently see is not positive). Your children will eventually conform to the words—remember, they should be spirit and life—that come out of your mouth. When you speak words that align with what God says about them, He will manifest those affirmations in their hearts!

Your Heavenly Father
will teach you
how to be a
"Good Father"
if you let Him.

CHAPTER 10

BE FREE

Shame can be humiliating and distressing due to the awareness of wrong or foolish behavior. Shame has hindered men in their fatherhood. The guilt and shame of past mistakes can play over and over in your head, leading you down a dreary road with no return. Fathers must embrace grace rather than condemnation, but you can only receive grace from God. The only way to benefit from this grace is to have a relationship with Jesus Christ. John 14:6 (KJV) says, "Jesus saith unto him, I am the way, the truth, and the life: no man cometh unto the Father, but by me."

One possible understanding of grace is "undeserved favour." Grace is often associated with the anointing. Having the anointing of God means having God's Spirit or presence upon you. We all need God's blessing, personally and as fathers, because it breaks the chains and lifts the burdens of the past, present, and future. Isaiah 10:27 (KJV) confirms this: "And it shall come to pass in that day, that his burden shall be taken away from off thy shoulder, and his yoke from off thy neck, and the yoke shall be destroyed because of the anointing." The anointing will set you free, and the grace of God will sustain you and propel you into your future.

Another interpretation of grace is to have "divine strength" from God. This divine strength enables you to have supernatural abilities that you don't naturally possess as a human being. It is necessary to have a relationship with God through Jesus Christ to access supernatural abilities from God. Sometimes it takes supernatural abilities to be a "Good Father." This is the only way for you to truly be liberated! I always tell people I want to be a "Good Father" because *He* is a "Good Father!" The Bible declares in Acts 17:28 (KJV), "For in him we live, and move, and have our being; as certain also of your poets have said, For we are also his offspring."

There are certain things that your natural instincts as a father might not lead you to do, but your spiritual side will guide you. Conviction in the spiritual realm is a positive thing. I understand that those who have been or are incarcerated may not like the word "conviction," but having a solid belief in your spirit will push you to do things outside your comfort zone. That is exactly where God wants you to be—outside of your comfort zone! He wants to shape you into the person and father He envisions, but you must let Him take complete control of your life. I feel in the spiritual realm that someone might say, "I don't need to do all of that as a father because I am already a good father." To that, I would say, don't be prideful, my brother, because no matter what level you are on as a father, God wants you to go deeper with Him, and there is something else He is trying to reveal to you as a father. Wow! I love it! We have the best teachers! Our Heavenly Father is the best teacher!

When we say we want to be a "Good Father" because He (God) is a "Good Father," this means our relationship with our children should resemble God's relationship with us. My question to you is, are you there yet? Are you on that level? I will answer it for you: No, we are not on that level, and we will never be, but we should strive to be who God called us to be as fathers to our children.

As you allow God to build a foundation within you and establish a relationship with Him, I would encourage you also to build a foundation with your children. Some may think you are already there, but you are not. Some of you are there and are ready to go to the next level. This process is humbling because you must look at yourself in the mirror and allow God to deal with you. If you have many cracks in your foundation and wonder why your relationship with your children isn't working, you must start from ground zero. Get rid of the old foundation and build a new one. That is where you will need the grace of God, as you won't be able to do this in your strength.

The foundation's purpose is to establish trust with your children. You might think, "My children already trust me." Your children may trust you in one area, but do they trust you in every area? Building trust in various areas will cultivate a relationship that will last a lifetime, which I work on every day. Honestly, your children may trust you one day and not trust you at all the next. You can't base the trust level on your children's feelings because they change daily. You have to base your trust level with your children on the foundation's strength.

When you build a house, the most important part is the foundation. Regardless of the weather, a strong foundation ensures the house stands firm. Similarly, as a "Good Father," investing effort in building a solid foundation for a stable relationship with your children is crucial. After establishing this foundation, it's advisable to seek a mentor who has proven to be a "Good Father" and follow his example to achieve similar results. Following the principles of building this foundation is essential; the final step is to embody the qualities of a "Good Father." Maintaining a relationship with God and operating in grace rather than the law makes it possible to repent, forgive, and make better decisions when mistakes are made.

As I conclude this book, I encourage you to be honest with yourself. You may be a father doing a great job being a "Good Father" to your children. You can check each box, but today, I encourage you to aim higher in God to be a "Great Father" and not just a "Good Father" to your children. You may be a "Good Father," but only half of the time. You might be doing great as a father, but you could be more focused more often. You may be a man who has a child and doesn't even acknowledge the child or your duties as a father. Unfortunately, I don't consider this to be good fathering but rather just being a biological dad. You are just a dad because your child was born. Yet, there is still hope for you! Wherever you decide to stand as a father, it will be time to deepen your relationship with your children, and most importantly, with Christ.

Throughout this book, I reference Jesus Christ multiple times. I invite you to accept Him as Lord and Savior.

Salvation (For those who desire to accept Jesus Christ for the first time)

Repeat after me:

Jesus, I accept You into my heart as my Lord and Savior. I surrender my life to You. I repent of my sins and turn my back on the world. I believe Jesus died on the cross for my sins. He was buried in a tomb, and God resurrected Him. I AM SAVED!

Rededication (For those who desire to rededicate their lives back to the Lord Jesus Christ)

Jesus, please forgive me for turning my back on You. I repent of my sins and turn my back on the world. I surrender my life to You. I rededicate my life back to You. I thank You for Your grace and mercy. Wash me with your blood, in Jesus' name, Amen.

BOOK SUMMARY

The "Good Father" is a redemption plan for fathers. The book shares how to be FREE from the guilt and shame of past mistakes during fatherhood. Tee Jay Woods gives practical steps (accepting grace, asking for forgiveness, and demonstrating "Good Father" characteristics) to be the "Good Father" God created every man to be!

As you read "The Good Father," embrace your "Good Father" identity, which manifests generational blessings instead of curses. As men adopt the "Good Father" mentality, communities will change, cities will change, regions will change, states will change, the country will change, and ultimately, the nation will change for the better!

AUTHOR'S BIO

Travis "Tee Jay" Woods, Jr. is an author speaker, trainer, licensed minister, father, husband, and servant of God! He also hosts the new live online show, "Unfiltered Conversations." Tee Jay is the founder and president of Youth Impact, a non-profit organization that has served youth for over eleven years.

Minister Tee Jay received a Bachelor's Degree in Business Marketing from Virginia State University in 2002. He received his Master's Degree in Human Services with a concentration in Marriage and Family Counseling from Liberty University in 2017.

Through his ministry, Minister Tee Jay has been showing people how to live a life of restoration rooted in Christ.

Made in the USA
Middletown, DE
24 January 2025